DAILY KINDNESS

DAILY

365 DAYS OF COMPASSION

KINDNESS

Photos and Wisdom to Enrich Your Spirit

NATIONAL GEOGRAPHIC

WASHINGTON, D.C.

Since 1888, the National Geographic Society has funded more than 12,000 research, exploration, and preservation projects around the world. National Geographic Partners distributes a portion of the funds it receives from your purchase to National Geographic Society to support programs including the conservation of animals and their habitats.

National Geographic Partners
1145 17th Street NW
Washington, DC 20036-4688 USA

Become a member of National Geographic and activate your benefits today at natgeo.com/jointoday.

For information about special discounts for bulk purchases, please contact National Geographic Books Special Sales: specialsales@natgeo.com

For rights or permissions inquiries, please contact National Geographic Books Subsidiary Rights: bookrights@natgeo.com

ISBN: 978-1-4262-1844-6

Interior design: Katie Olsen and Callie Bonaccorsy

Printed in China

17/PPS/1

JANUARY
RESPECT

JANUARY 1

If it is not right do not do it;
if it is not true do not say it.

~ MARCUS AURELIUS

What I want is so simple I almost
can't say it: elementary kindness.

~ BARBARA KINGSOLVER

I think there's just one kind of folks.
Folks.

~ HARPER LEE

JANUARY 4

Each one of us matters, has a role to play, and makes
a difference. Each one of us must take responsibility
for our own lives, and above all, show respect and love
for living things around us, especially each other.

~ JANE GOODALL

JANUARY 5

When you are content
to be simply yourself
and don't compare
or compete, everyone
will respect you.

~ LAO-TZU

January 6

Watching great people do what you love
is a good way to start learning
how to do it yourself.

~ Amy Poehler

What's terrible is to pretend that second-rate
is first-rate. To pretend that you don't need love
when you do; or you like your work when
you know quite well you're capable of better.

~ DORIS LESSING

JANUARY 8

To free us from the expectations of others,
to give us back to ourselves—there lies
the great, the singular power of self-respect.

~ JOAN DIDION

JANUARY 9

The truth is humbling, terrifying, and often exhilarating. It blows the doors off the hinges and fills the world with fresh air.

~ AUGUSTEN BURROUGHS

January 10

If you want to be
respected by others,
the great thing is
to respect yourself.
Only by that, only by
self-respect will you
compel others
to respect you.

~ Fyodor Dostoyevsky

Speak with integrity. Say only what you mean. Avoid using the word to speak against yourself or to gossip about others. Use the power of your word in the direction of truth and love.

~ Don Miguel Ruiz

January 12

All I'm saying is, kindness
don't have no boundaries.

~ Kathryn Stockett

January 13

This is my simple religion. There is no need for
temples; no need for complicated philosophy.
Our own brain, our own heart is our temple;
the philosophy is kindness.

~ Dalai Lama XIV

When you come right down to it,
the secret of having it all is loving it all.

~ JOYCE BROTHERS

JANUARY 15

Our lives are not our own. From womb
to tomb, we are bound to others.
Past and present, and by each crime
and every kindness, we birth our future.

~ DAVID MITCHELL

I don't see how you can respect yourself
if you must look in the hearts and
minds of others for your happiness.

~ HUNTER S. THOMPSON

JANUARY 17

Simple, genuine goodness is the best capital
to found the business of this life upon. It lasts
when fame and money fail, and is the only riches
we can take out of this world with us.

~ LOUISA MAY ALCOTT

January 18

You must live life with the full knowledge
that your actions will remain.
We are creatures of consequence.

~ Zadie Smith

Value yourself more.

~ OPRAH WINFREY

Always do right. This will gratify
some people and astonish the rest.

~ MARK TWAIN

JANUARY 21

Love can often be misguided and do as much
harm as good, but respect can do only good.
It assumes that the other person's stature
is as large as one's own, his rights
as reasonable, his needs as important.

~ ELEANOR ROOSEVELT

JANUARY 22

Good thoughts and
actions can never
produce bad results.
Bad thoughts and
actions can never
produce good results.

~ JAMES ALLEN

JANUARY 23

When we approach with reverence,
great things decide to approach us.

~ JOHN O'DONOHUE

JANUARY 24

Raise your words, not voice.
It is rain that grows flowers,
not thunder.

~ RUMI

In the long run, the sharpest weapon
of all is a kind and gentle spirit.

~ ANNE FRANK

You your best thing . . . You are.

~ TONI MORRISON

JANUARY 27

The worst thing:
to give yourself away
in exchange for
not enough love.

~ JOYCE CAROL OATES

JANUARY 28

To belittle, you have
to be little.

~ Kahlil Gibran

Love is not something we give or get; it is something that we nurture and grow, a connection that can only be cultivated between two people when it exists within each one of them—we can only love others as much as we love ourselves.

~ BRENÉ BROWN

January 30

You will never say to yourself
when you are old, *Ah, I wish
I was not good to that person.*
You will never think that.

~ Khaled Hosseini

Mutual caring relationships require
kindness and patience, tolerance,
optimism, joy in the other's achievements,
confidence in oneself, and the ability
to give without undue thought of gain.

~ FRED ROGERS

FEBRUARY

AFFECTION

FEBRUARY 1

Affection is responsible for nine-tenths
of whatever solid and durable happiness
there is in our natural lives.

~ C. S. LEWIS

FEBRUARY 2

One is loved because one is loved.
No reason is needed for loving.

~ PAULO COELHO

FEBRUARY 3

You can search throughout the entire universe
for someone who is more deserving of your love
and affection than you are yourself, and that
person is not to be found anywhere. You, yourself,
as much as anybody in the entire universe,
deserve your love and affection.

~ BUDDHA

To get the full value of joy you must
have someone to divide it with.

~ MARK TWAIN

FEBRUARY 5

People are felt
rather than seen
after the first
few moments.

~ JOHN STEINBECK

Only love can be divided endlessly
and still not diminish.

~ ANNE MORROW LINDBERGH

Life must be rich and full
of loving—it's no good otherwise,
no good at all, for anyone.

~ JACK KEROUAC

FEBRUARY 8

Love is not a because, it's a no matter what.

~ JODI PICOULT

Nobody has ever measured,
even the poets, how much
a heart can hold.

~ ZELDA FITZGERALD

Love isn't a state of perfect caring. It is an active noun like struggle. To love someone is to strive to accept that person exactly the way he or she is, right here and now.

~ Fred Rogers

FEBRUARY 11

To love or have loved, that is enough.

~ Victor Hugo

You'll find, my friend, that what
you love will take you places
you never dreamed you'd go.

~ TONY KUSHNER

FEBRUARY 13

That best portion of a good man's life;
His little, nameless, unremembered acts
Of kindness and of love.

~ WILLIAM WORDSWORTH

Love is the feeling we have for those we care deeply about and hold in high regard. It can be light as the hug we give a friend or heavy as the sacrifices we make for our children.

~ CHERYL STRAYED

We cannot tell the precise moment when friendship is formed. As in filling a vessel drop by drop, there is at last a drop which makes it run over; so in a series of kindnesses there is at least one which makes the heart run over.

~ RAY BRADBURY

FEBRUARY 16

There is nothing in the world
so irresistibly contagious as
laughter and good humor.

~ CHARLES DICKENS

February 17

It's quite simple: It is only with the heart
that one can see rightly; what is essential
is invisible to the eyes.

~ Antoine de Saint-Exupéry

Love is to people what
water is to plants.

~ MARIANNE WILLIAMSON

Talk not of
wasted affection;
affection never
was wasted.

~ HENRY WADSWORTH
LONGFELLOW

When we're connected to others,
we become better people.

~ RANDY PAUSCH

FEBRUARY 21

Emotions, in my experience,
aren't covered by single words.

~ JEFFREY EUGENIDES

February 22

Let us love, since that is all
our hearts were made for.

~ St. Thérèse de Lisieux

Very young children are not afraid to express
what they feel. They are so loving that if they
perceive love, they melt into love. They are not
afraid to love at all. That is the description
of a normal human being.

~ DON MIGUEL RUIZ

FEBRUARY 24

The thing about
light is that it really
isn't yours; it's
what you gather
and shine back.

~ ANNE LAMOTT

We can live without religion and
meditation, but we cannot survive
without human affection.

~ DALAI LAMA XIV

FEBRUARY 26

Guard well within yourself that treasure,
kindness. Know how to give without
hesitation, how to lose without regret,
how to acquire without meanness.

~ GEORGE SAND

FEBRUARY 27

Love doesn't just sit there, like a stone,
it has to be made, like bread;
remade all the time, made new.

~ URSULA K. LE GUIN

Spread love everywhere you go.
Let no one ever come to you
without leaving happier.

~ MOTHER TERESA

MARCH
AUTHENTICITY

Authenticity is a collection of choices that
we have to make every day. It's about the choice
to show up and be real. The choice to be honest.
The choice to let our true selves be seen.

~ Brené Brown

March 2

Only the truth of who you are,
if realized, will set you free.

~ Eckhart Tolle

MARCH 3

The most fundamental aggression to ourselves,
the most fundamental harm we can do
to ourselves, is to remain ignorant by not
having the courage and the respect to look
at ourselves honestly and gently.

~ PEMA CHÖDRÖN

Do your thing and don't care
if they like it.

~ TINA FEY

MARCH 5

The most authentic
thing about us is our
capacity to create, to
overcome, to endure,
to transform, to love
and to be greater
than our suffering.

~ BEN OKRI

MARCH 6

The privilege of a lifetime
is being who you are.

~ JOSEPH CAMPBELL

As we let our own light shine,
we unconsciously give other people
permission to do the same.

~ MARIANNE WILLIAMSON

We are what we pretend to be,
so we must be careful about
what we pretend to be.

~ KURT VONNEGUT

March 9

Don't become something just because someone
else wants you to, or because it's easy;
you won't be happy. You have to do what
you really, really, really, really want to do,
even if it scares the shit out of you.

~ Kristen Wiig

MARCH 10

The summit of happiness is reached
when a person is ready to be what he is.

~ DESIDERIUS ERASMUS

MARCH 11

What draws people to be friends
is that they see the same truth.
They share it.

~ C. S. LEWIS

Don't worry about being good . . .
Aspire to be authentic.

~ YANN MARTEL

You prefer to be natural? Sometimes.
But it is such a very difficult pose
to keep up.

~ OSCAR WILDE

MARCH 14

Be brave. Be authentic.
Practice saying the
word "love" to the
people you love
so when it matters
the most to say it,
you will.

~ CHERYL STRAYED

MARCH 15

Our deeds determine us, as much
as we determine our deeds.

~ GEORGE ELIOT

Do not ask what the world needs.
Ask what makes you come alive and go
do that. Because what the world needs
is people who have come alive.

~ HOWARD THURMAN

MARCH 17

If you don't know what
you love, you are lost.

~ HARUKI MURAKAMI

This above all: to thine
own self be true.

~ WILLIAM SHAKESPEARE

The free soul is rare, but you know it when
you see it—basically because you feel good,
very good, when you are near or with them.

~ CHARLES BUKOWSKI

March 20

If every tiny flower wanted to be a rose,
spring would lose its loveliness.

~ St. Thérèse de Lisieux

In trying to please all,
he had pleased none.

~ AESOP

MARCH 22

The essence of
being human is
that one does not
seek perfection.

~ GEORGE ORWELL

Let us say what we feel, and feel what
we say; let speech harmonize with life.

~ SENECA

March 24

I know but one freedom, and that
is the freedom of the mind.

~ Antoine de Saint-Exupéry

March 25

The most exhausting thing in life,
I have discovered, is being insincere.

~ Anne Morrow Lindbergh

Insist on yourself.

~ RALPH WALDO EMERSON

MARCH 27

Love cannot be forced,
love cannot be coaxed
or teased. It comes out
of heaven, unasked
and unsought.

~ PEARL S. BUCK

The very least you can do in your life
is figure out what you hope for.
And the most you can do is live inside
that hope. Not admire it from a distance
but live right in it, under its roof.

~ BARBARA KINGSOLVER

MARCH 29

Accept who you are;
and revel in it.

~ MITCH ALBOM

MARCH 30

Everything in the universe
is within you.
Ask all from yourself.

~ RUMI

The greatest thing in the world is to know
how to belong to oneself.

~ MICHEL DE MONTAIGNE

APRIL

SERENITY

April 1

Peace is present right here and now, in ourselves
and in everything we do and see . . . Every breath
we take, every step we take, can be filled
with peace, joy, and serenity . . . The question is
whether or not we are in touch with it. We need
only to be awake, alive in the present moment.

~ Thich Nhat Hanh

Don't be too quick to draw
conclusions from what happens
to you; simply let it happen.

~ RAINER MARIA RILKE

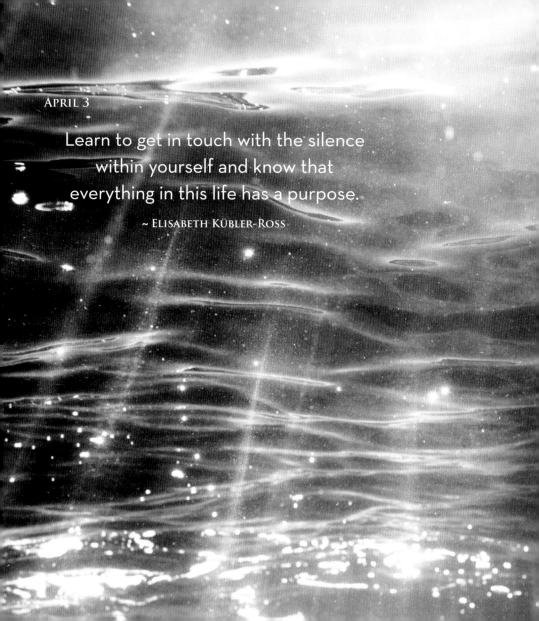

Learn to get in touch with the silence
within yourself and know that
everything in this life has a purpose.

~ ELISABETH KÜBLER-ROSS

APRIL 4

Life is a series of natural and spontaneous changes.
Don't resist them; that only creates sorrow.
Let reality be reality. Let things flow naturally
forward in whatever way they like.

~ LAO-TZU

April 5

You've got to learn to do everything lightly . . .
Yes, feel lightly even though you're
feeling deeply. Just lightly let things
happen and lightly cope with them.

~ Aldous Huxley

Read, or sit in revery and watch the
changing colors of the waves that break
upon the idle seashore of the mind.

~ HENRY WADSWORTH LONGFELLOW

You must take life
the way it comes
at you and make
the best of it.

~ YANN MARTEL

APRIL 8

Our work for peace must begin within
the private world of each one of us.

~ DAG HAMMARSKJÖLD

Never let the future disturb you. You will meet it,
if you have to, with the same weapons of reason
which today arm you against the present.

~ MARCUS AURELIUS

Peace is always beautiful.

~ WALT WHITMAN

April 11

In order to understand the world,
one has to turn away from it
on occasion.

~ Albert Camus

APRIL 12

Rivers know this: there is no hurry.
We shall get there someday.

~ A. A. MILNE

You have to be where you are
to get where you need to go.

~ AMY POEHLER

APRIL 14

There is no way to peace,
peace is the way.

~ MAHATMA GANDHI

APRIL 15

We place a happy life in
a tranquility of mind.

~ MARCUS TULLIUS CICERO

Least effort is expended when our actions
are motivated by love, because nature
is held together by the energy of love.

~ DEEPAK CHOPRA

Either peace or happiness,
let it enfold you.

~ CHARLES BUKOWSKI

APRIL 18

Those who are free of resentful
thoughts surely find peace.

~ BUDDHA

The only place
the mind will ever
find peace is
inside the silence
of the heart.
That's where
you need to go.

~ ELIZABETH GILBERT

It is good to have an end to journey toward;
but it is the journey that matters, in the end.

~ URSULA K. LE GUIN

April 21

Finish each day and be done with it. You have done what you could. Some blunders and absurdities no doubt crept in; forget them as soon as you can. Tomorrow is a new day.

~ Ralph Waldo Emerson

APRIL 22

If we have no peace, it is because we have
forgotten that we belong to each other.

~ MOTHER TERESA

APRIL 23

Peace comes from within.
Do not seek it without.

~ BUDDHA

Learn to be quiet enough to hear
the sound of the genuine within yourself
so that you can hear it in other people.

~ MARIAN WRIGHT EDELMAN

APRIL 25

There is no greatness where there is
not simplicity, goodness, and truth.

~ LEO TOLSTOY

APRIL 26

Change is one thing.
Acceptance is another.

~ ARUNDHATI ROY

APRIL 27

Recompense injury with justice, and
recompense kindness with kindness.

~ CONFUCIUS

Serenity comes from the ability
to say "Yes" to existence.

~ AYN RAND

A happy life must be to a great extent
a quiet life, for it is only in an atmosphere
of quiet that true joy can live.

~ BERTRAND RUSSELL

APRIL 30

We do not need to go out and find love; rather,
we need to be still and let love discover us.

~ JOHN O'DONOHUE

MAY

EMPATHY

MAY 1

Compassion is not a relationship between
healer and the wounded. It's a relationship
between equals. Only when we know our
own darkness well can we be present
with the darkness of others.

~ PEMA CHÖDRÖN

MAY 2

The only way we will survive is by being kind.
The only way we can get by in this world
is through the help we receive from others.
No one can do it alone, no matter
how great the machines are.

~ AMY POEHLER

MAY 3

In time we often become one with those
we once failed to understand.

~ PATTI SMITH

Remember that everyone you meet
is afraid of something, loves something
and has lost something.

~ H. JACKSON BROWN, JR.

Every one of us is,
in the cosmic
perspective, precious.
If a human disagrees
with you, let him live.
In a hundred billion
galaxies, you will
not find another.

~ CARL SAGAN

There is a wisdom of the Head . . .
there is a wisdom of the Heart.

~ CHARLES DICKENS

MAY 7

Compassion is an unstable emotion.
It needs to be translated into action,
or it withers.

~ SUSAN SONTAG

MAY 8

One is never fortunate or as
unfortunate as one imagines.

~ FRANÇOIS DE LA ROCHEFOUCAULD

People must learn to hate, and if they can learn to hate, they can be taught to love, for love comes more naturally to the human heart than its opposite.

~ NELSON MANDELA

MAY 10

Everyone behaves
badly . . . Give them
a proper chance.

~ ERNEST HEMINGWAY

The story of human intimacy is one
of constantly allowing ourselves to see
those we love most deeply in a new,
more fractured light. Look hard. Risk that.

~ CHERYL STRAYED

I am driven by two main philosophies: know more today about the world than I knew yesterday and lessen the suffering of others. You'd be surprised how far that gets you.

~ NEIL deGRASSE TYSON

MAY 13

I will not say: do not weep;
for not all tears are an evil.

~ J. R. R. TOLKIEN

The really important kind of freedom involves
attention, and awareness, and discipline, and
effort, and being able truly to care about other
people and to sacrifice for them, over and over,
in myriad petty little unsexy ways, every day.

~ DAVID FOSTER WALLACE

MAY 15

If you send out goodness from yourself,
or if you share that which is happy or good
within you, it will all come back to you multiplied
ten thousand times . . . The more love you
give away, the more love you will have.

~ JOHN O'DONOHUE

When someone is crying, of course, the noble
thing to do is to comfort them. But if someone
is trying to hide their tears, it may also be noble
to pretend you do not notice them.

~ LEMONY SNICKET

MAY 17

We have two ears and one mouth
so that we can listen twice
as much as we speak.

~ EPICTETUS

We have so far to go to realize our
human potential for compassion,
altruism, and love.

~ JANE GOODALL

MAY 19

Love and compassion are necessities,
not luxuries. Without them, humanity
cannot survive.

~ DALAI LAMA XIV

MAY 20

If you see someone
without a smile, give
them one of yours.

~ DOLLY PARTON

We don't set out to save the world;
we set out to wonder how other people
are doing and to reflect on how our
actions affect other people's hearts.

~ PEMA CHÖDRÖN

MAY 22

Those who do not weep,
do not see.

~ VICTOR HUGO

The highest forms of understanding
we can achieve are laughter
and human compassion.

~ RICHARD FEYNMAN

MAY 24

You can either practice being right
or practice being kind.

~ ANNE LAMOTT

May 25

You can only
understand people
if you feel them
in yourself.

~ John Steinbeck

MAY 26

A man sees in the world what
he carries in his heart.

~ Johann Wolfgang von Goethe

You never really understand a person until you consider things from his point of view . . . Until you climb inside of his skin and walk around in it.

~ HARPER LEE

It's a little embarrassing
that after 45 years of
research and study,
the best advice
I can give people
is to be a little kinder
to each other.

~ ALDOUS HUXLEY

MAY 29

Never be so busy as not
to think of others.

~ MOTHER TERESA

MAY 30

You think your pain and your heartbreak
are unprecedented in the history of the world,
but then you read. It was Dostoevsky and
Dickens who taught me that the things
that tormented me most were the very things
that connected me with all the people who
were alive, or who had ever been alive.

~ JAMES BALDWIN

Many people need desperately to receive
this message: "I feel and think much as you do,
care about many of the things you care about,
although most people do not care about them.
You are not alone."

~ KURT VONNEGUT

JUNE

MINDFULNESS

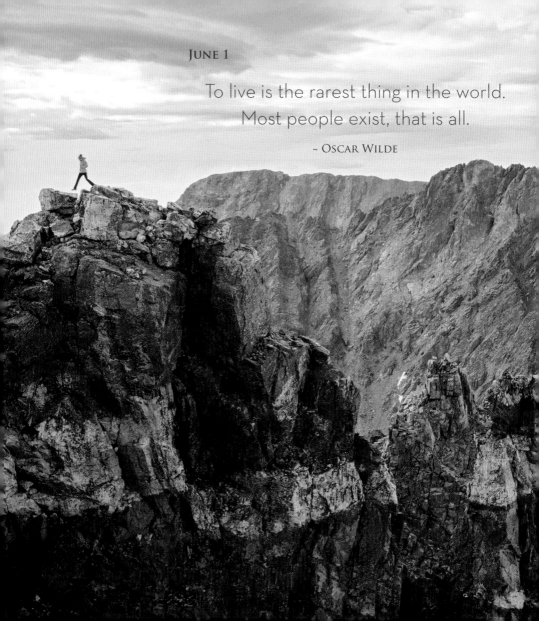

JUNE 1

To live is the rarest thing in the world.
Most people exist, that is all.

~ OSCAR WILDE

June 2

The aim of life is to live, and to live
means to be aware, joyously,
drunkenly, serenely, divinely aware.

~ Henry Miller

Love isn't something natural. Rather it
requires discipline, concentration, patience,
faith, and the overcoming of narcissism.
It isn't a feeling, it is a practice.

~ ERICH FROMM

The more clearly we can focus our
attention on the wonders and realities
of the universe about us, the less taste
we shall have for destruction.

~ RACHEL CARSON

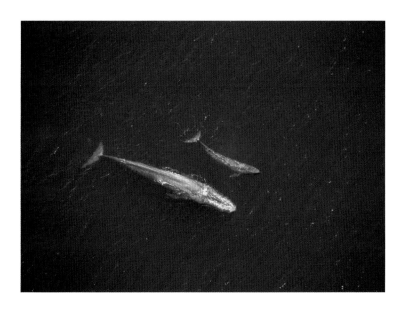

JUNE 5

And I asked myself
about the present:
how wide it was,
how deep it was,
how much was mine
to keep.

~ KURT VONNEGUT

June 6

Taking in the good, whenever
and wherever we find it, gives us
new eyes for seeing and living.

~ Krista Tippett

In mindfulness one is not only restful
and happy, but alert and awake.
Meditation is not evasion; it is
a serene encounter with reality.

~ THICH NHAT HANH

Be fully in the moment, open yourself to the
powerful energies dancing around you.

~ ERNEST HEMINGWAY

JUNE 9

Set wide the window.
Let me drink the day.

~ EDITH WHARTON

JUNE 10

The happiness of
your life depends
upon the quality of
your thoughts.

~ MARCUS AURELIUS

The more you look,
the more you see.

~ ROBERT M. PIRSIG

Look at everything as though
you were seeing it for either the first
or last time. Then your time on earth
will be filled with glory.

~ BETTY SMITH

JUNE 13

Nothing behind me,
everything ahead of me,
as is ever so on the road.

~ JACK KEROUAC

JUNE 14

Consciously put your attention in the heart
and ask your heart what to do.

~ DEEPAK CHOPRA

JUNE 15

It is our choices, Harry,
that show what we truly are,
far more than our abilities.

~ J. K. ROWLING

Realize deeply that the present
moment is all you ever have.

~ ECKHART TOLLE

June 17

If something is going to happen
to me, I want to be there.

~ Albert Camus

JUNE 18

We can only be said to be alive
in those moments when our hearts
are conscious of our treasures.

~ THORNTON WILDER

For there is never anything but the
present, and if one cannot live there,
one cannot live anywhere.

~ ALAN WATTS

The purpose of our life
needs to be positive.
We weren't born with
the purpose of causing
trouble, harming others.
For our life to be
of value . . . we must
develop basic good
human qualities—warmth,
kindness, compassion.
Then our life becomes
meaningful and more
peaceful—happier.

~ DALAI LAMA XIV

Love is the essential existential fact.
It is our ultimate reality and our purpose
on earth. To be consciously aware of it,
to experience love in ourselves
and others, is the meaning of life.

~ Marianne Williamson

June 22

There is still a lot to learn, and there
is always great stuff out there.
Even mistakes can be wonderful.

~ Robin Williams

JUNE 23

Perhaps the most "spiritual" thing
any of us can do is simply to look through
our own eyes, see with eyes of wholeness,
and act with integrity and kindness.

~ JON KABAT-ZINN

Nothing ever becomes real
till it is experienced.

~ JOHN KEATS

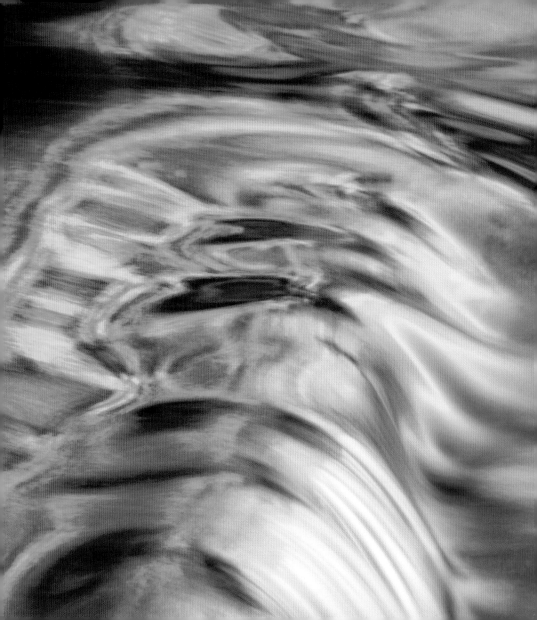

JUNE 25

The measure of your life
is the amount of beauty
and happiness of which
you are aware.

~ AGNES MARTIN

All that happens means something;
nothing you do is ever insignificant.

~ ALDOUS HUXLEY

JUNE 27

It takes courage . . . to endure the sharp pains
of self discovery rather than choose to take
the dull pain of unconsciousness that
would last the rest of our lives.

~ MARIANNE WILLIAMSON

JUNE 28

Most of the time, all you have is
the moment and the imperfect love
of the people around you.

~ ANNE LAMOTT

Isn't it wonderful the way the world
holds both the deeply serious,
and the unexpectedly mirthful?

~ MARY OLIVER

You need to learn how
to select your thoughts
just the same way
you select your
clothes every day.
This is a power
you can cultivate.

~ ELIZABETH GILBERT

JULY
PATIENCE

July 1

Imperfect love must not be condemned
and rejected but made perfect. The way
is always forward, never back.

~ Iris Murdoch

How poor are they that have not patience!
What wound did ever heal but by degrees?

~ WILLIAM SHAKESPEARE

Nothing ever goes away until it has
taught us what we need to know.

~ PEMA CHÖDRÖN

JULY 4

I am still in the process of
growing up, but I will make
no progress if I lose any
of myself along the way.

~ MADELEINE L'ENGLE

JULY 5

Know your own happiness. You want
nothing but patience; or give it a more
fascinating name: call it hope.

~ JANE AUSTEN

There is nothing stronger than
these two: patience and time,
they will do it all.

~ LEO TOLSTOY

JULY 7

We could never
learn to be brave
and patient if
there were only joy
in the world.

~ HELEN KELLER

JULY 8

Just be quiet and patient. Let evil and unpleasantness
pass quietly over you. Do not try to avoid them.
On the contrary, observe them carefully. Let active
understanding take the place of reflex irritation, and
you will grow out of your trouble. Men can achieve
greatness only by surmounting their own littleness.

~ FRANZ KAFKA

Think well of all, be patient with all,
and try to find the good in all.

~ MUHAMMAD ALI

JULY 10

What good is the warmth without cold
to give it sweetness?

~ JOHN STEINBECK

July 11

We do know that no one gets wise enough
to really understand the heart of another,
though it is the task of our life to try.

~ Louise Erdrich

Patience is needed
with everyone,
but first of all
with ourselves.

~ St. Francis de Sales

JULY 13

Of all the hardships a person had
to face, none was more punishing
than the simple act of waiting.

~ KHALED HOSSEINI

Experience is what you get when you didn't
get what you wanted. And experience is often
the most valuable thing you have to offer.

~ RANDY PAUSCH

Adventures do occur, but not punctually . . .
Life never gives us what we want at the
moment that we consider appropriate.

~ E. M. FORSTER

JULY 16

Patience is bitter, but its fruit is sweet.

~ JEAN-JACQUES ROUSSEAU

JULY 17

Some lessons can't be taught,
they simply have to be learned.

~ JODI PICOULT

Without patience, we will learn less in life.
We will see less. We will feel less.

~ MOTHER TERESA

Muddy water is
best cleared by
leaving it alone.

~ ALAN WATTS

JULY 20

Kindness is in our power,
even when fondness is not.

~ SAMUEL JOHNSON

Adopt the pace of Nature.
Her secret is patience.

~ RALPH WALDO EMERSON

So much of this was patience—waiting,
and thinking and doing things right.
So much of all this, so much of all living
was patience and thinking.

~ GARY PAULSEN

JULY 23

Have patience with everything that
remains unsolved in your heart.

~ RAINER MARIA RILKE

JULY 24

Nothing great is
produced suddenly.

~ EPICTETUS

JULY 25

Drop by drop is the pitcher filled.

~ BUDDHA

July 26

All human wisdom is summed up
in two words—wait and hope.

~ ALEXANDRE DUMAS

JULY 27

Patience is also a form of action.

~ AUGUSTE RODIN

JULY 28

Cleverness is good, patience is better.

~ HERMANN HESSE

If it is right, it happens—
The main thing is not to hurry.
Nothing good gets away.

~ JOHN STEINBECK

In the end, in search of useful wisdom,
you could only come back to the most
hackneyed concepts, like kindness,
forbearance, infinite patience.

~ CHAD HARBACH

July 31

Patience, patience, patience, is what the
sea teaches. Patience and faith. One should
lie empty, open, choiceless as a beach—
waiting for a gift from the sea.

~ Anne Morrow Lindbergh

AUGUST

ENCOURAGEMENT

AUGUST 1

Beautiful things are difficult.

~ PLATO

I do not at all understand the mystery
of grace—only that it meets us where we are
but does not leave us where it found us.

~ ANNE LAMOTT

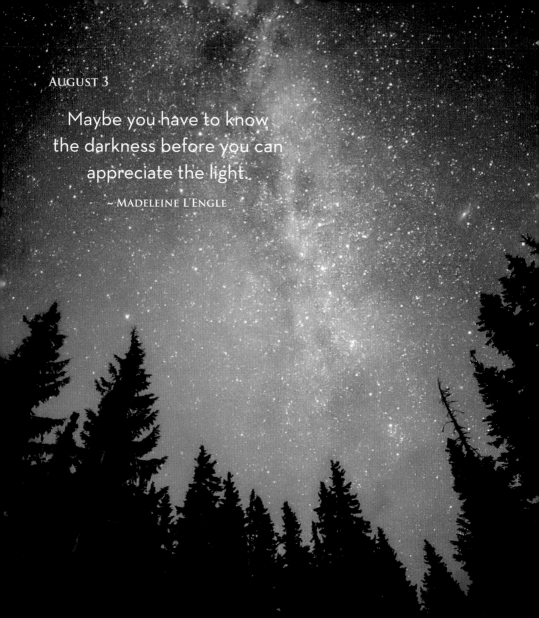

Maybe you have to know
the darkness before you can
appreciate the light.

~ MADELEINE L'ENGLE

AUGUST 4

All of us are just holding it together in various
ways—and that's okay, and we just need
to go easy with one another, knowing that
we're all these incredibly fragile beings.

~ ALAIN DE BOTTON

August 5

You can't be that kid standing at the
top of the waterslide, overthinking it.
You have to go down the chute.

~ Tina Fey

It's universally accepted that children need love,
but at what age are people supposed
to stop needing it? We never do. We need
love in order to live happily, as much as
we need oxygen in order to live at all.

~ MARIANNE WILLIAMSON

AUGUST 7

There is no passion to be
found playing small—
in settling for a life that
is less than the one you
are capable of living.

~ NELSON MANDELA

And now that you don't have to
be perfect, you can be good.

~ JOHN STEINBECK

AUGUST 9

None of us knows what might happen even
the next minute, yet still we go forward.

~ PAULO COELHO

Never doubt that you are valuable
and deserving of every chance and
opportunity in the world to pursue
and achieve your own dreams.

~ HILLARY CLINTON

Wonder. Go on and wonder.

~ WILLIAM FAULKNER

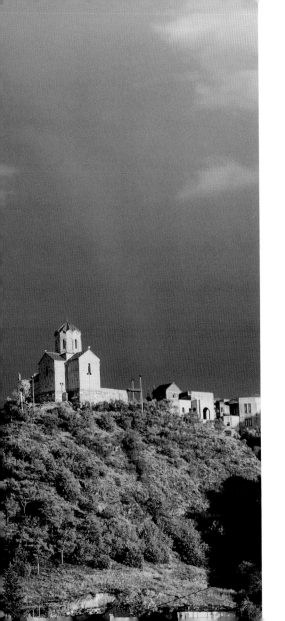

August 12

Try to be a rainbow
in someone's cloud.

~ Maya Angelou

There are times to stay put, and what
you want will come to you, and there
are times to go out into the world and
find such a thing for yourself.

~ LEMONY SNICKET

Never give up on what you really
want to do. The person with big
dreams is more powerful than
one with all the facts.

~ H. JACKSON BROWN, JR.

AUGUST 15

Every limit is a beginning as
well as an ending.

~ GEORGE ELIOT

AUGUST 16

It is not in doing what you like,
but in liking what you do that
is the secret of happiness.

~ J. M. BARRIE

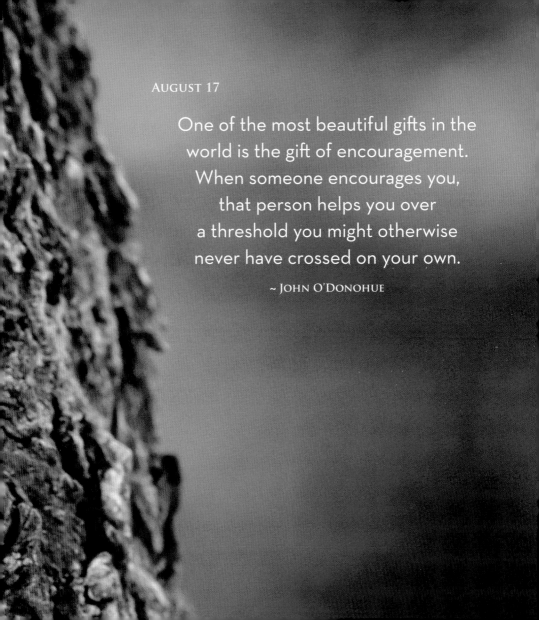

One of the most beautiful gifts in the
world is the gift of encouragement.
When someone encourages you,
that person helps you over
a threshold you might otherwise
never have crossed on your own.

~ JOHN O'DONOHUE

AUGUST 18

It's your life—but only if you make it so.

~ ELEANOR ROOSEVELT

AUGUST 19

Instruction does much, but
encouragement everything.

~ JOHANN WOLFGANG VON GOETHE

August 20

Hope springs forever.

~ J. K. Rowling

One may go a long way
after one is tired.

~ FRENCH PROVERB

Don't worry about it.
The right thing
will come at
the right time.

~ DANIELLE STEEL

August 23

To love another human in all of her splendor
and imperfect perfection, it is a magnificent
task . . . tremendous and foolish and human.

~ Louise Erdrich

If the dream is held close to the heart, and
imagination is applied to what there is close
at hand, everything is still possible.

~ ROBERT FULGHUM

Carry out a random act of kindness,
with no expectation of reward, safe in
the knowledge that one day someone
might do the same for you.

~ DIANA SPENCER, PRINCESS OF WALES

August 26

Begin with that most frightening of all things, a clean slate. And then look, every day, at the choices you are making, and when you ask yourself why you are making them, find this answer: Because they are what I want, or wish for. Because they reflect who and what I am.

~ Anna Quindlen

August 27

Nothing is a waste
of time if you use the
experience wisely.

~ Auguste Rodin

Practice random kindness and
senseless acts of beauty.

~ ANNE HERBERT

You do it because the doing of it is the thing.
The doing is the thing. The talking and
worrying and thinking is not the thing.

~ AMY POEHLER

AUGUST 30

Nothing happens until something moves.

~ ALBERT EINSTEIN

Constant kindness can accomplish much.
As the sun makes ice melt, kindness
causes misunderstanding, mistrust,
and hostility to evaporate.

~ ALBERT SCHWEITZER

SEPTEMBER

VULNERABILITY

SEPTEMBER 1

To be fully seen by somebody, then, and
be loved anyhow—this is a human offering
that can border on miraculous.

~ ELIZABETH GILBERT

SEPTEMBER 2

The only way to find true happiness is
to risk being completely cut open.

~ CHUCK PALAHNIUK

September 3

It's gonna hurt because it matters.

~ John Green

We cultivate love when we allow our most vulnerable and powerful selves to be deeply seen and known, and when we honor the spiritual connection that grows from that offering with trust, respect, kindness, and affection.

~ BRENÉ BROWN

SEPTEMBER 5

A person is, among all
else, a material thing,
easily torn and
not easily mended.

~ IAN MCEWAN

Most important and most vulnerable
of human emotions: Love.

~ PAULO COELHO

Let yourself be gutted. Let it
open you. Start here.

~ CHERYL STRAYED

Love is the burning point of life, and since all life
is sorrowful, so is love. The stronger the love,
the more the pain. Love itself is pain,
you might say—the pain of being truly alive.

~ JOSEPH CAMPBELL

SEPTEMBER 9

To be alive at all is to have scars.

~ JOHN STEINBECK

Love is the opposite of power.
That's why we fear it so much.

~ GREGORY DAVID ROBERTS

If you don't understand, ask questions. If you're uncomfortable about asking questions, say you are uncomfortable about asking questions and then ask anyway. It's easy to tell when a question is coming from a good place. Then listen some more. Sometimes people just want to feel heard.

~ CHIMAMANDA NGOZI ADICHIE

SEPTEMBER 12

Find the courage to ask questions and to express what you really want. Communicate with others as clearly as you can to avoid misunderstandings, sadness, and drama.

~ Don Miguel Ruiz

Avoiding danger is no safer in the long run
than outright exposure. Life is either
a daring adventure or nothing.

~ HELEN KELLER

SEPTEMBER 14

The moment that you feel that, just possibly,
you're walking down the street naked,
exposing too much of your heart and
your mind and what exists on the inside,
showing too much of yourself. That's the
moment you may be starting to get it right.

~ NEIL GAIMAN

September 15

You are so weak. Give up to grace. /
The ocean takes care of each wave till
it gets to shore. / You need more
help than you know.

~ Rumi

It's impossible to live without failing
at something—unless you live so cautiously
that you might as well not have lived at all—
in which case you have failed by default.

~ J. K. ROWLING

To love at all is to be vulnerable.

~ C. S. LEWIS

SEPTEMBER 18

There is no intensity of love or feeling that
does not involve the risk of crippling hurt.
It is a duty to take this risk, to love and
feel without defense or reserve.

~ WILLIAM S. BURROUGHS

SEPTEMBER 19

We need never
be ashamed of
our tears.

~ CHARLES DICKENS

September 20

We can't be brave without fear.

~ Muhammad Ali

What is really hard, and really amazing,
is giving up on being perfect and beginning
the work of becoming yourself.

~ ANNA QUINDLEN

It is through weakness and
vulnerability that most of us learn
empathy and compassion and
discover our soul.

~ DESMOND TUTU

September 23

You have to love. You have to feel.
It is the reason you are here on earth.
You are here to risk your heart. You are
here to be swallowed up.

~ Louise Erdrich

SEPTEMBER 24

The only thing that makes life possible
is permanent, intolerable uncertainty:
not knowing what comes next.

~ URSULA K. LE GUIN

When we were children, we used to think that when we were grown-up we would no longer be vulnerable. But to grow up is to accept vulnerability . . . to be alive is to be vulnerable.

~ MADELEINE L'ENGLE

What happens
when people open
their hearts?
They get better.

~ HARUKI MURAKAMI

September 27

Opening your heart and being courageous and
telling people that you care about them or like them
or that you think they're special only makes you
a better, bigger, kinder, softer, more loving person
and only attracts more love in your life.

~ Amy Poehler

Out of your vulnerabilities
will come your strength.

~ SIGMUND FREUD

Learn to trust what you cannot see
far more than what you can see.

~ CAROLINE MYSS

SEPTEMBER 30

You cannot live when you are
untouchable. Life is vulnerability.

~ ÉDOUARD BOUBAT

OCTOBER

GENEROSITY

October 1

The place to improve the world is first
in one's own heart and head and hands,
and then work outward from there.

~ Robert M. Pirsig

Be kind whenever possible.
It is always possible.

~ DALAI LAMA XIV

OCTOBER 3

When one loves,
one does not calculate.

~ ST. THÉRÈSE DE LISIEUX

OCTOBER 4

How wonderful it is that nobody
need wait a single moment before
starting to improve the world.

~ ANNE FRANK

October 5

It is well to give
when asked, but it is
better to give unasked,
through understanding;
and to the open-handed
the search for one who
shall receive is joy
greater than giving.

~ Kahlil Gibran

OCTOBER 6

You will learn a lot about yourself if you stretch
in the direction of goodness, of bigness, of
kindness, of forgiveness, of emotional bravery.

~ CHERYL STRAYED

OCTOBER 7

For it is in giving that we receive.

~ ST. FRANCIS OF ASSISI

October 8

To serve is beautiful, but only if it is done
with joy and a whole heart and a free mind.

~ Pearl S. Buck

Try to learn to let what is unfair teach you.

~ DAVID FOSTER WALLACE

OCTOBER 10

If you look for perfection,
you'll never be content.

~ LEO TOLSTOY

OCTOBER 11

Attention is the rarest and
purest form of generosity.

~ SIMONE WEIL

OCTOBER 12

While we do our good works let us not forget
that the real solution lies in a world in which
charity will have become unnecessary.

~ CHINUA ACHEBE

OCTOBER 13

Real generosity towards the future lies
in giving all to the present.

~ ALBERT CAMUS

Go out and do for others what
somebody did for you.

~ RANDY PAUSCH

OCTOBER 15

It is higher and nobler
to be kind.

~ MARK TWAIN

The heart that gives, gathers.

~ LAO-TZU

OCTOBER 17

Love is always a choice.

~ GARY CHAPMAN

OCTOBER 18

Kindness is good will.
Kindness says, "I want
you to be happy."

~ J. H. RANDOLPH RAY

OCTOBER 19

The enjoyment comes from knowing the
receiver understands the spirit of the gift.

~ OPRAH WINFREY

If you're feeling helpless,
help someone.

~ AUNG SAN SUU KYI

OCTOBER 21

It is every man's obligation to put
back into the world at least the
equivalent of what he takes out of it.

~ ALBERT EINSTEIN

OCTOBER 22

We can only learn
to love by loving.

~ IRIS MURDOCH

OCTOBER 23

You will make all kinds of mistakes; but as
long as you are generous and true and
also fierce you cannot hurt the world
or even seriously distress her.

~ WINSTON CHURCHILL

All of us want to do well. But if we
do not do good, too, then doing well
will never be enough.

~ ANNA QUINDLEN

It is no way to live, to wait to love.

~ DAVE EGGERS

OCTOBER 26

What will matter is the good we did, not the
good we expected others to do.

~ ELIZABETH LESSER

OCTOBER 27

Sometimes self-
interested is the
most generous thing
you can be.

~ TONY KUSHNER

OCTOBER 28

A kind word is like a spring day.

~ RUSSIAN PROVERB

You do not become good by trying
to be good, but by finding the goodness
that is already within you, and allowing
that goodness to emerge.

~ ECKHART TOLLE

OCTOBER 30

Always try to be a little kinder
than is necessary.

~ J. M. BARRIE

OCTOBER 31

Do your little bit of good where you are;
it's those little bits of good put together
that overwhelm the world.

~ DESMOND TUTU

November

STRENGTH

NOVEMBER 1

Don't find fault; find a remedy.

~ HENRY FORD

November 2

In order for us to liberate the energy
of our strength, our weakness must
first have a chance to reveal itself.

~ Paulo Coelho

November 3

We are each responsible for our own life.
If you're holding anyone else accountable
for your happiness, you're wasting your time.
You must be fearless enough to give yourself
the love you didn't receive.

~ Oprah Winfrey

NOVEMBER 4

Take pride in your pain . . .
you are stronger than
those who have none.

~ LOIS LOWRY

You must not ever stop being whimsical.
And you must not, ever, give anyone else
the responsibility for your life.

~ MARY OLIVER

NOVEMBER 6

You have power over your mind—
not outside events. Realize this,
and you will find strength.

~ MARCUS AURELIUS

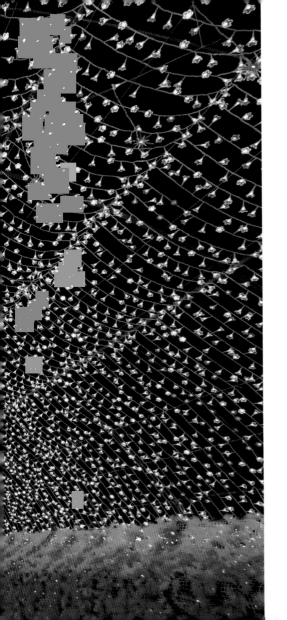

NOVEMBER 7

In yourself right now
is all the place
you've got.

~ FLANNERY O'CONNOR

Between grief and nothing
I will take grief.

~ WILLIAM FAULKNER

NOVEMBER 9

In a world as wrong as this one, all we
can do is make things as right as we can.

~ BARBARA KINGSOLVER

November 10

Be strong. Live honorably
and with dignity. When you
don't think you can, hold on.

~ James Frey

NOVEMBER 11

Love is a possible strength
in an actual weakness.

~ THOMAS HARDY

NOVEMBER 12

Sometimes the worst thing that happens to you,
the thing you think you can't survive . . . it's the thing
that makes you better than you used to be.

~ JENNIFER WEINER

You can't be brave if you've only had
wonderful things happen to you.

~ MARY TYLER MOORE

NOVEMBER 14

Nothing is so strong as gentleness,
nothing so gentle as real strength.

~ ST. FRANCIS DE SALES

NOVEMBER 15

Develop the strength to do bold things,
not the strength to suffer.

~ NICCOLÒ MACHIAVELLI

NOVEMBER 16

You can accomplish
by kindness what you
cannot by force.

~ PUBLILIUS SYRUS

Good actions give strength to ourselves
and inspire good actions in others.

~ PLATO

NOVEMBER 18

It's one of the secrets of strength: We're so
much more likely to find it in the service
of others than in service to ourselves.

~ DAVID LEVITHAN

NOVEMBER 19

So please ask yourself:
What would I do
if I weren't afraid?
And then go do it.

~ SHERYL SANDBERG

November 20

Courage is not something that you already have
that makes you brave when the tough times start.
Courage is what you earn when you've been
through the tough times and you discover
they aren't so tough after all.

~ MALCOLM GLADWELL

You gain strength, courage, and confidence
by every experience in which you really stop
to look fear in the face. You are able to say
to yourself, "I have lived through this horror.
I can take the next thing that comes along." . . .
You must do the thing you think you cannot do.

~ ELEANOR ROOSEVELT

Whatever happens to you belongs to you.
Make it yours. Feed it to yourself even
if it feels impossible to swallow. Let it
nurture you, because it will.

~ CHERYL STRAYED

Do your best and trust that others do their best.
And be faithful in small things because
it is in them that your strength lies.

~ MOTHER TERESA

NOVEMBER 24

Those who hope,
by retiring from
the world, to earn
a holiday from human
frailty, in themselves
and others, are usually
disappointed.

~ IRIS MURDOCH

It is the small everyday deeds of
ordinary folk that keep the darkness
at bay. Small acts of kindness and love.

~ J. R. R. TOLKIEN

NOVEMBER 26

There are two ways of exerting one's
strength; one is pushing down,
the other is pulling up.

~ BOOKER T. WASHINGTON

November 27

To hurt is as human as to breathe.

~ J. K. Rowling

I read somewhere how important
it is in life not necessarily to be
strong . . . but to feel strong.

~ JON KRAKAUER

The world breaks everyone
and afterward many are strong
at the broken places.

~ ERNEST HEMINGWAY

NOVEMBER 30

Always remember you are braver than
you believe, stronger than you seem,
and smarter than you think.

~ A. A. MILNE

DECEMBER

GRATITUDE

December 1

Reflect upon your present blessings—of
which every man has many—not on your past
misfortunes, of which all men have some.

~ Charles Dickens

December 2

Thanks for this day, for all birds safe in
their nests, for whatever this is, for life.

~ Barbara Kingsolver

December 3

Appreciation is a wonderful thing.
It makes what is excellent in others
belong to us as well.

~ Voltaire

I have often done the little I could to correct
the stale trick of taking things for granted:
all the more because it is not even taking them
for granted. It is taking them without gratitude;
that is, emphatically as not granted.

~ G. K. CHESTERTON

December 5

We already have
everything we need.

~ Pema Chödrön

DECEMBER 6

Acknowledging the good that you already have
in your life is the foundation for all abundance.

~ ECKHART TOLLE

DECEMBER 7

Remember that very little is
needed to make a happy life.

~ MARCUS AURELIUS

As we express our gratitude, we must never forget that the highest appreciation is not to utter words, but to live by them.

~ JOHN F. KENNEDY

DECEMBER 9

I urge you to please notice when you are happy
and exclaim or murmur or think at some point,
"if this isn't nice, I don't know what is."

~ KURT VONNEGUT

DECEMBER 10

Do not despise your
own place and hour.
Every place is
under the stars.
Every place is the
center of the world.

~ JOHN BURROUGHS

Most human beings have an almost infinite
capacity for taking things for granted.

~ ALDOUS HUXLEY

The simple things are also the
most extraordinary things,
and only the wise can see them.

~ PAULO COELHO

DECEMBER 13

The true way to live is to enjoy every moment
as it passes, and surely it is in the everyday
things around us that the beauty of life lies.

~ LAURA INGALLS WILDER

DECEMBER 14

Showing gratitude is one
of the simplest yet most
powerful things humans
can do for each other.

~ RANDY PAUSCH

Gratitude can transform any situation.
It alters your vibration moving you
from negative energy to positive.

~ OPRAH WINFREY

DECEMBER 16

Never forget that all you have
is all you need.

~ SARAH BAN BREATHNACH

DECEMBER 17

If you look the right way,
you can see that the
whole world is a garden.

~ FRANCES HODGSON BURNETT

Let us be grateful to the people who make us happy; they are the charming gardeners who make our souls blossom.

~ MARCEL PROUST

DECEMBER 19

All sanity depends on this: that it should be
a delight to feel the roughness of a carpet under
smooth soles, a delight to feel heat strike the skin,
a delight to stand upright, knowing the bones
are moving easily under the flesh.

~ DORIS LESSING

DECEMBER 20

In the end, though, maybe we must all give up trying to pay back the people in this world who sustain our lives. In the end, maybe it's wiser to surrender before the miraculous scope of human generosity and to just keep saying thank you, forever and sincerely, for as long as we have voices.

~ ELIZABETH GILBERT

Cultivate the habit of being grateful for every good thing that comes to you, and to give thanks continuously. And because all things have contributed to your advancement, you should include all things in your gratitude.

~ Wallace D. Wattles

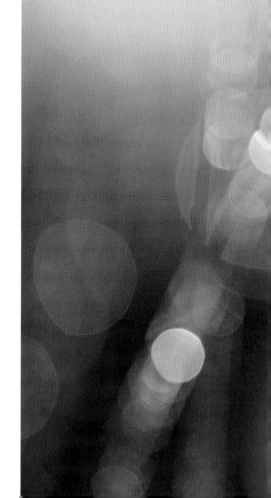

December 22

Nothing has
happened today
except kindness.

~ Gertrude Stein

December 23

What you must do is this: Rejoice evermore.
Pray without ceasing. In everything give thanks.
I am not all the way capable of so much,
but those are the right instructions.

~ Wendell Berry

If the only prayer you said in your whole life was, "thank you," that would suffice.

~ MEISTER ECKEHART

Gratitude can transform common days into thanksgivings, turn routine jobs into joy, and change ordinary opportunities into blessings.

~ WILLIAM ARTHUR WARD

December 26

Kindness, kindness, kindness.

~ Susan Sontag

DECEMBER 27

Let gratitude be the
pillow upon which you
kneel to say your nightly
prayer. And let faith be
the bridge you build
to overcome evil
and welcome good.

~ MAYA ANGELOU

Gratitude begins in our hearts and then dovetails
into behavior. It almost always makes you willing
to be of service, which is where the joy resides.

~ ANNE LAMOTT

December 29

Gratitude is looking on the brighter side of life,
even if it means hurting your eyes.

~ Ellen DeGeneres

DECEMBER 30

Gratitude is not only the greatest of virtues,
but the parent of all others.

~ MARCUS TULLIUS CICERO

Here is the world, and you live in it, and
are grateful. You try to be grateful.

~ MICHAEL CUNNINGHAM

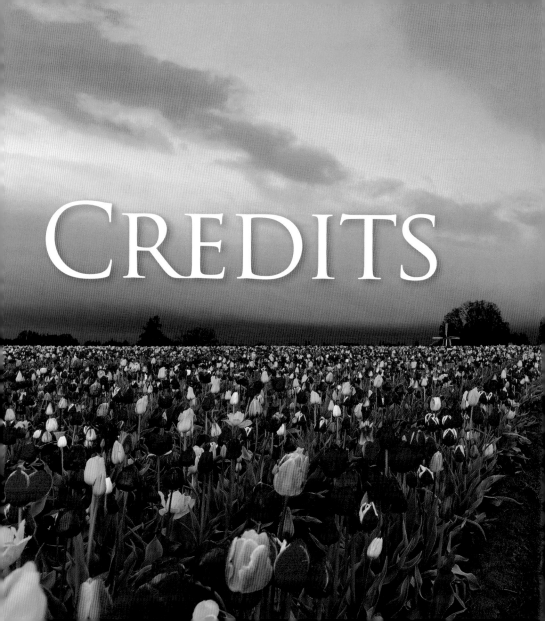

CREDITS

CONTRIBUTOR INDEX

Chödrön, Pema (Deirdre Blomfield-Brown)
b. 1936
American teacher, author, and Tibetan Buddhist nun

Chopra, Deepak
b. 1947
Indian medical doctor and spiritual writer

Churchill, Winston Spencer
1874–1965
British prime minister and statesman

Cicero, Marcus Tullius
106–43 B.C.
Roman philosopher, statesman, and orator

Clinton, Hillary Rodham
b. 1947
American politician

Coelho, Paulo
b. 1947
Brazilian novelist and lyricist

Confucius
551–479 B.C.
Chinese philosopher and teacher

Cunningham, Michael
b. 1952
American novelist and screenwriter

D

Dalai Lama XIV (Lhamo Dondrub)
b. 1935
Tibetan spiritual and political leader

DeGeneres, Ellen Lee
b. 1958
American comedian and television host

Dickens, Charles
1812–1870
English writer and social critic

Didion, Joan
b. 1934
American journalist and novelist

Dostoyevsky, Fyodor Mikhaylovich
1821–1881
Russian novelist, short-story writer, and essayist

Dumas, Alexandre
1802–1870
French playwright, historian, and author

E

Eckehart, Meister
1260–1327
German theologian and philosopher

Edelman, Marian Wright
b. 1939
American activist

Eggers, Dave
b. 1970
American writer, editor, and publisher

Einstein, Albert
1879–1955
German-American theoretical physicist

Eliot, George (Mary Ann Evans)
1819–1880
British novelist

Emerson, Ralph Waldo
1803–1882
American essayist, lecturer, and poet

Epictetus
A.D. 55–135
Greek sage and Stoic philosopher

Erasmus, Desiderius
1466–1536
Dutch humanist, social critic, and theologian

Erdrich, Louise
b. 1954
Native American writer

Eugenides, Jeffrey
b. 1960
American novelist and short story writer

F

Faulkner, William
1897–1962
American writer

Fey, Tina (Elizabeth Stamatina)
b. 1970
American actress, comedian, writer, and producer

Feynman, Richard Phillips
1918–1988
American theoretical physicist

Fitzgerald, Zelda
1900–1948
American novelist

Ford, Henry
1863–1947
American industrialist, inventor, and entrepreneur

Forster, E. M. (Edward Morgan)
1879–1970
British novelist, essayist, and critic

Frank, Anne
1929–1945
German diarist

Freud, Sigmund
1856–1939
Austrian neurologist and father of psychoanalysis

Frey, James Christopher
b. 1969
American writer

Fromm, Erich
1900–1980
German-American social psychologist and psychoanalyst

Fulghum, Robert Lee
b. 1937
American author and minister

G

Gaiman, Neil Richard MacKinnon
b. 1960
English author

Gandhi, Mohandas
Karamchand (Mahatma)
1869–1948
Indian civil rights leader

Gibran, Kahlil
1883–1931
Lebanese-American
artist, poet, writer,
and philosopher

Gilbert, Elizabeth
b. 1969
American writer

Gladwell, Malcolm
b. 1963
Canadian journalist
and author

Goethe, Johann
Wolfgang von
1749–1832
German novelist,
poet, playwright,
and philosopher

Goodall, Jane
b. 1934
British primatologist
and anthropologist

Green, John
b. 1977
American author

H

Hammarskjöld, Dag
1905–1961
Swedish diplomat,
economist, and author

Hanh, Thich Nhat
b. 1926
Vietnamese Buddhist
monk, poet, author,
and activist

Harbach, Chad
b. 1975
American writer

Hardy, Thomas
1840–1928
English novelist and
poet

Hemingway, Ernest
1899–1961
American author
and journalist

Herbert, Anne
b. 1952
American writer

Hesse, Hermann
1877–1962
German-Swiss
poet, novelist,
and painter

Hosseini, Khaled
b. 1965
Afghan-born
American novelist
and physician

Hugo, Victor
1802–1885
French poet, novelist,
and dramatist

Huxley, Aldous
(Leonard)
1894–1963
British novelist,
playwright, and
satirist

J

Johnson, Samuel
1709–1784
British poet, essayist,
literary critic, and
lexicographer

K

Kabat-Zinn, Jon
b. 1944
American scientist,
writer, and professor

Kafka, Franz
1883–1924
Austro-Hungarian
novelist

Keats, John
1795–1821
British poet

Keller, Helen
1880–1968
American writer,
lecturer, and activist

Kennedy, John
Fitzgerald
1917–1963
American president

Kerouac, Jack
1922–1969
American novelist
and poet

King, Martin Luther, Jr.
1929–1968
American clergyman,
activist, and leader

Kingsolver, Barbara
b. 1955
American novelist,
poet, and essayist

Krakauer, Jon
b. 1954
American writer

Kübler-Ross, Elisabeth
1926–2004
American psychiatrist
and author

Kushner, Tony (Anthony
Robert)
b. 1956
American playwright
and screenwriter

L

Lamott, Anne
b. 1954
American novelist and
nonfiction writer

Lao-tzu
604–531 B.C.
Chinese philosopher

La Rochefoucauld,
François de
1613–1680
French memoirist
and writer

Lee, Harper
1926–2016
American novelist

Le Guin, Ursula K.
b. 1929
American novelist,
poet, essayist

L'Engle, Madeleine
1918–2007
American novelist

Lesser, Elizabeth
b. 1952
American author

Lessing, Doris
1919–2013
British novelist
and poet

Levithan, David
b. 1972
American author
and editor

Lewis, C. S. (Clive Staples)
1898–1963
Irish novelist, scholar, and broadcaster

Lindbergh, Anne Morrow
1906–2001
American writer, poet, and aviator

Longfellow, Henry Wadsworth
1807–1882
American poet

Lowry, Lois
b. 1937
American children's writer

M

Machiavelli, Niccolò
1469–1527
Italian philosopher, diplomat, and writer

Mandela, Nelson
1918–2013
South African president

Martel, Yann
b. 1963
Canadian author

Martin, Agnes Bernice
1912–2004
Canadian-American artist

McEwan, Ian
b. 1948
English novelist and screenwriter

Miller, Henry
1891–1980
American novelist

Milne, A. A. (Alan Alexander)
1882–1956
English novelist, poet, and playwright

Mitchell, David
b. 1969
English novelist

Montaigne, Michel de
1533–1592
French writer and philosopher

Moore, Mary Tyler
1936–2017
American actress

Morrison, Toni (Chloe Wofford)
b. 1931
American novelist and poet

Murakami, Haruki
b. 1949
Japanese writer

Murdoch, Iris
1919–1999
British novelist and philosopher

Myss, Caroline
b. 1952
American author

O

Oates, Joyce Carol
b. 1938
American author

O'Connor, (Mary) Flannery
1925–1964
American writer and essayist

O'Donohue, John
1956–2008
Irish poet, philosopher, and Catholic scholar

Okri, Ben
b. 1959
Nigerian poet and novelist

Oliver, Mary
b. 1935
American poet

Orwell, George (Eric Arthur Blair)
1903–1950
British novelist and journalist

P

Palahniuk, Chuck
b. 1962
American novelist

Parton, Dolly
b. 1946
American singer-songwriter

Paulsen, Gary
b. 1939
American children's author

Pausch, Randy (Randolph Frederick)
1960–2008
American professor

Picoult, Jodi
b. 1966
American author

Pirsig, Robert (Maynard)
1928–2017
American author and philosopher

Plato
428–348 B.C.
Ancient Greek philosopher

Poehler, Amy Meredith
b. 1971
American actress, comedian, and author

Proust, Marcel
1871–1922
French novelist

Q

Quindlen, Anna
b. 1952
American journalist and novelist

R

Rand, Ayn
1905–1982
American novelist

Ray, J. H. (Jackson Harvelle) Randolph
1886–1963
American author and priest

Rilke, Rainer Maria
1875–1926
Bohemian Austrian poet

Roberts, Gregory David
b. 1952
Australian author

Rodin, Auguste
1840–1917
French sculptor

Rogers, Frederick McFeely
1928–2003
American educator and television personality

Roosevelt, (Anna) Eleanor
1884–1962
American first lady, activist, and author

Rousseau, Jean-Jacques
1712–1778
Swiss philosopher and writer

Rowling, J. K. (Joanne Kathleen)
b. 1965
British novelist

Roy, Arundhati (Suzanna)
b. 1961
Indian author and political activist

Ruiz, Don Miguel
b. 1952
Mexican author

Rumi (Jalal ad-Din ar-Rumi)
1207–1273
Persian poet

Russell, Bertrand
1872–1970
British philosopher, mathematician, and social critic

S

Sagan, Carl
1934–1996
American astronomer, astrophysicist, and author

Saint-Exupéry, Antoine de
1900–1944
French author, poet, and aviator

Sales, St. Francis de
1567–1622
Bishop of Geneva

Sand, George (Amandine-Aurore-Lucile Dupin)
1804–1876
French novelist and memoirist

Sandberg, Sheryl
b. 1969
American businesswoman

Schweitzer, Albert
1875–1965
German and French philosopher, musician, and physician

Seneca, Lucius Annaeus
4 B.C.–A.D. 65
Roman philosopher, statesman, and dramatist

Shakespeare, William
1564–1616
British playwright and poet

Smith, Betty
1896–1972
American novelist

Smith, Patti
b. 1946
American singer-songwriter, poet, and artist

Smith, Zadie
b. 1975
English author

Snicket, Lemony (Daniel Handler)
b. 1970
American author

Sontag, Susan
1933–2004
American writer and teacher

Spencer, Diana
1961–1997
Wife of Charles, Prince of Wales, and international humanitarian

Steel, Danielle
b. 1947
American novelist

Stein, Gertrude
1874–1946
American novelist and poet

Steinbeck, John
1902–1968
American novelist

Stockett, Kathryn
b. 1969
American novelist

Strayed, Cheryl
b. 1968
American author

Suu Kyi, Aung San
b. 1945
Burmese politician, diplomat, and author

Syrus, Publilius
85–43 B.C.
Latin writer

T

Teresa, Mother (Agnes Gonxha Bojaxhiu)
1910–1997
Albanian-Indian nun and religious leader

Thérèse de Lisieux, St.
1873–1897
French Carmelite nun

Thompson, Hunter S.
1937–2005
American journalist and author

Thurman, Howard
1899–1981
American author, theologian, and civil rights leader

Tippett, Krista
b. 1960
American journalist, author, and entrepreneur

Tolkien, J. R. R. (John Ronald Reuel)
1892–1973
English writer, poet, and professor

Tolle, Eckhart
b. 1948
German spiritual teacher and writer

Tolstoy, Leo
1828–1910
Russian novelist and short-story writer

Tutu, Desmond
b. 1931
South African religious leader and antiapartheid activist

Twain, Mark (Samuel Langhorne Clemens)
1835–1910
American novelist and humorist

Tyson, Neil deGrasse
b. 1958
American astrophysicist, cosmologist, author, and educator

V

Voltaire (François-Marie Arouet)
1694–1778
French writer, playwright, and philosopher

Vonnegut, Kurt
1922–2007
American writer

W

Wallace, David Foster
1962–2008
American author and professor

Ward, William Arthur
1921–1994
American inspirational writer and poet

Washington, Booker T.
1856–1915
American educator, activist, author, and political leader

Wattles, Wallace (Delois)
1860–1911
American author

Watts, Alan (Wilson)
1915–1973
British philosopher, writer, and speaker

Weil, Simone
1909–1943
French philosopher and social activist

Weiner, Jennifer
b. 1970
American writer

Wharton, Edith (Newbold Jones)
1862–1937
American novelist

Whitman, Walt
1819–1892
American poet, essayist, and journalist

Wiig, Kristen (Carroll)
b. 1973
American actress and comedian

Wilde, Oscar
1854–1900
Irish novelist and dramatist

Wilder, Laura Ingalls
1867–1957
American author

Wilder, Thornton
1897–1975
American playwright and novelist

Williams, Robin (McLaurin)
1951–2014
American comedian and actor

Williamson, Marianne
b. 1952
American spiritual writer and poet

Winfrey, Oprah
b. 1954
American media personality

Wordsworth, William
1770–1850
English poet

ILLUSTRATIONS CREDITS

Cover, Rosemary Calvert/Getty Images; 1, Butterfly Hunter/Shutterstock; 2-3, Elena Leonova/Getty Images; 5, Vitaly Titov/Shutterstock.

January

Opener, Pal Teravagimov Photography/Getty Images; 1, StevanZZ/Shutterstock; 2, Aleksandrs Samuilovs/Shutterstock; 3, Xavier Arnau/Getty Images; 4, Anup Shah/Getty Images; 5, Valery Sidelnykov/Shutterstock; 6, elnavegante/Getty Images; 7, Shebeko/Shutterstock; 8, tomgigabite/Shutterstock; 9, Leonid Ikan/Shutterstock; 10, freebilly/Getty Images; 11, erashov/Shutterstock; 12, Joseph De Sciose/Getty Images; 13, Tzido/Getty Images; 14, Ev Thomas/Shutterstock; 15, littleny/Shutterstock; 16, Africa Studio/Shutterstock; 17, Kichigin/Shutterstock; 18, cunfek/Getty Images; 19, Viktor Kuchin/Shutterstock; 20, James Brey/Getty Images; 21, Jimmy Tran/Shutterstock; 22, wingmar/Getty Images; 23, Boris Stroujko/Shutterstock; 24, stanley45/Getty Images; 25, Melory/Shutterstock; 26, Elena Grama/Shutterstock; 27, Peter Adams/Getty Images; 28, Imran Kadir Photography/Getty Images; 29, bearacreative/Shutterstock; 30, Elena Elisseeva/Shutterstock; 31, Leonid Ikan/Shutterstock.

February

Opener, Anya Berkut/Getty Images; 1, Anurak Pongpatimet/Shutterstock; 2, kisklau/Shutterstock; 3, Anton Jankovoy/Shutterstock; 4, Ruth Black/Shutterstock; 5, Tatyana Tomsickova/Getty Images; 6, snowturtle/Shutterstock; 7, Peter Wey/Shutterstock; 8, Nadia Cruzova/Shutterstock; 9, Mandy Disher Photography/Getty Images; 10, Alena Ozerova/Shutterstock; 11, Roman Mikhailiuk/Shutterstock; 12, Zoonar/N. Sorokin/Getty Images; 13, sunsinger/Shutterstock; 14, Nailia Schwarz/Shutterstock; 15, Yellowj/Shutterstock; 16, ahudson216/Shutterstock; 17, Ronald Sumners/Shutterstock; 18, Phichet Chaiyabin/Shutterstock; 19, E.A. Janes/Getty Images; 20, chuyuss/Shutterstock; 21, Nan Zhong/Getty Images; 22, Krunja/Shutterstock; 23, Vilor/Shutterstock; 24, Jumpstart Studios/Getty Images; 25, My Good Images/Shutterstock; 26, Hayati

Kayhan/Shutterstock; 27, Julia Sudnitskaya/Shutterstock; 28/29, muratart/Shutterstock.

March

Opener, vtwinpixel/Getty Images; 1, Alexey Yuzhakov/Shutterstock; 2, John Lund/Getty Images; 3, Kurit Afsheen/Getty Images; 4, Viktor Zadorozhnyi/Shutterstock; 5, Lukas Gojda/Shutterstock; 6, seewhatmitchsee/Getty Images; 7, Pushish Images/Shutterstock; 8, DNY59/Getty Images; 9, Arnaud Bertrande/Getty Images; 10, anshar/Shutterstock; 11, Mark Bridger/Shutterstock; 12, djgis/Shutterstock; 13, Andrea Haase/Dreamstime.com; 14, Johnny Adolphson/Shutterstock; 15, S. Borisov/Shutterstock; 16, Tropical studio/Shutterstock; 17, LANStudios/Shutterstock; 18, Elena Kharichkina/Shutterstock; 19, tichr/Shutterstock; 20, S_Photo/Shutterstock; 21, mmac72/Getty Images; 22, Andrew Mayovskyy/Shutterstock; 23, Marian Weyo/Shutterstock; 24, gyn9037/Shutterstock; 25, Willyam Bradberry/Shutterstock; 26, Doidam 10/Shutterstock; 27, Stuart Dee/Getty Images; 28, kavram/Shutterstock; 29, aliasemma/Shutterstock; 30, Anatolii Vasilev/Shutterstock; 31, oatawa/Shutterstock.

April

Opener, Tomas Sereda/Getty Images; 1, Matteo Colombo/Getty Images; 2, nikamata/Getty Images; 3, Alexander Rhind/Getty Images; 4, Elena Belozorova/Shutterstock; 5, Smileus/Shutterstock; 6, pp1/Shutterstock; 7, kavalenkava/Shutterstock; 8, Napat/Shutterstock; 9, Michael Nichols/National Geographic Creative; 10, Uliana Bazar; 11, DNY59/Getty Images; 12, David Yarrow Photography/Getty Images; 13, Krakozawr/Getty Images; 14, apiguide/Shutterstock; 15, LordRunar/Getty Images; 16, Chris Johns/National Geographic Creative; 17, Maria Kraynova/Shutterstock; 18, MO_SES Premium/Shutterstock; 19, Bruce Dale/National Geographic Creative; 20, Irina Tischenko/Shutterstock; 21, Jupiter Images/Getty Images; 22, Sam Abell/National Geographic Creative; 23, Ingrid Prats/Shutterstock; 24, SJ Travel Photo and Video/Shutterstock.com; 25, Life

On White/Oxford Scientific/Getty Images; 26, Jan Bussan/Shutterstock; 27, Brenda Carson/Shutterstock; 28, Wojciech Lisinski/Shutterstock; 29, Shaiith/Shutterstock; 30, Elena Belozorova/Shutterstock.

MAY

Opener, Petermooy/Getty Images; 1, JOAT/Shutterstock; 2, Krisztian Farkas/Shutterstock; 3, Preto Perola/Shutterstock; 4, Michael Nichols/National Geographic Creative; 5, Bob Stefko/Getty Images; 6, Lev Kropotov/Shutterstock; 7, Dimitrios/Shutterstock; 8, Pacos Rulz/Getty Images; 9, Vladimir Melnik/Shutterstock; 10, Michael Nichols/National Geographic Creative; 11, Karin Broekhuijsen/Buiten-beeld/Minden Pictures/Getty Images; 12, Andrea Haase/Shutterstock; 13, mchin/Shutterstock; 14, idizimage/Getty Images; 15, StevanZZ/Shutterstock; 16, Shaiith/Shutterstock; 17, EcoPrint/Shutterstock; 18, Steve Raymer/National Geographic Creative; 19, Wasu Watcharadachaphong/Shutterstock; 20, Xidong Luo/Shutterstock; 21, Filip Fuxa/Shutterstock; 22, Kichigin/Shutterstock; 23, David Alan Harvey/National Geographic Creative; 24, Kati Molin/Shutterstock; 25, Roman Khomlyak/Shutterstock; 26, FooTToo/Shutterstock; 27, blew_i/Getty Images; 28, Quang Ho/Shutterstock; 29, Aleksandar Nakic/Getty Images; 30, Stokkete/Shutterstock; 31, Milosz_G/Shutterstock.

JUNE

Opener, Frank Krahmer/Getty Images; 1, Matt Propert; 2, Michael Forsberg/National Geographic Creative; 3, Vladimir Serov/Getty Images; 4, Patricio Robles Gil/Sierra Madre/Minden Pictures/Getty Images; 5, wingmar/Getty Images; 6, seawhisper/Shutterstock; 7, Ioana Catalina E/Shutterstock; 8, bernardo69/Getty Images; 9, Maya Kruchankova/Shutterstock; 10, Viacheslav Lopatin/Shutterstock.com; 11, Irina Tischenko/Shutterstock; 12, Walter Meayers Edwards/National Geographic Creative; 13, John Lund/Getty Images; 14, sunipix55/Shutterstock; 15, Ondrej Prosicky/Shutterstock; 16, nbiebach/Shutterstock; 17, Sergio Pitamitz/National Geographic Creative; 18, Valeriy Evlakhov/Shutterstock; 19, Adriana Varela Photography/Getty Images; 20, Markus Gebauer/Shutterstock; 21, tinnanut/Shutterstock; 22, welcomia/Shutterstock; 23, Iakov Kalinin/Getty Images; 24, Eakkachai2520/Shutterstock; 25,

Dean Pennala/Shutterstock; 26, Natalia Klenova/Shutterstock; 27, Ondrej Prosicky/Shutterstock; 28, Johan Swanepoel/Shutterstock; 29, Westend61/Getty Images; 30, Ignacio Gonzalez/Shutterstock.

JULY

Opener, Tomas Sereda/Getty Images; 1, Darrell Gulin/Getty Images; 2, pio3/Shutterstock; 3, Katsuaki Shoda/EyeEm/Getty Images; 4, Xuanlu Wang/Shutterstock; 5, Anna Bogush/Shutterstock; 6, Nor Gal/Shutterstock; 7, Peter Zelei Images/Getty Images; 8, Ditty_about_summer/Shutterstock; 9, Matt Propert; 10, Matt Propert; 11, aopsan/Shutterstock; 12, kavalenkava/Shutterstock; 13, Doug Lemke/Shutterstock; 14, chckyong/Getty Images; 15, Spaces Images/Getty Images; 16, 5 second Studio/Shutterstock; 17, 4Max/Shutterstock; 18, TFoxFoto/Shutterstock; 19, dszc/Getty Images; 20, baona/Getty Images; 21, OGphoto/Getty Images; 22, Roxana Bashyrova/Shutterstock; 23, luminouslens/Shutterstock; 24, Piriya Photography/Getty Images; 25, panphai/Shutterstock; 26, Matt Propert; 27, Doug Chinnery/Getty Images; 28, RT Images/Shutterstock; 29, Alena Haurylik/Shutterstock; 30, sssss1gmel/Getty Images; 31, Jag_cz/Getty Images.

AUGUST

Opener, Pictureguy/Shutterstock; 1, Marco Introini/Shutterstock; 2, Fippzor/Shutterstock; 3, Andrey Prokhorov/Shutterstock; 4, Chayse Sly/EyeEm/Getty Images; 5, Aleksey Stemmer/Shutterstock; 6, Fuse/Getty Images; 7, Werner Van Steen/Getty Images; 8, GracefulFoto/Shutterstock; 9, Nataliia Budianska/Shutterstock; 10, Ondrej Prosicky/Shutterstock; 11, John Fan Photography/Getty Images; 12, vvvita/Getty Images; 13, pixhook/Getty Images; 14, Photograph by Sarah Orsag/Getty Images; 15, Phil Schermeister/National Geographic Creative; 16, Jaroslaw Pawlak/Shutterstock; 17, Ondrej Prosicky/Shutterstock; 18, Kelly Sillaste/Getty Images; 19, Sirapob Horien/Shutterstock; 20, sevenke/Shutterstock; 21, antb/Shutterstock; 22, ArtTomCat/Shutterstock; 23, ZenShui/Michele Constantini/Getty Images; 24, kwasny221/Getty Images; 25, Alexander Raths/Shutterstock; 26, Taiga/Shutterstock; 27, Joseph Kim/Shutterstock; 28, SUN-FLOWER/Shutterstock; 29, Ian Sanderson/Getty Images; 30, Yan Balczewski/Shutterstock; 31, Galyna Andrushko/Shutterstock.

September

Opener, Levente Bodo/Getty Images; 1, Nick Brundle Photography/Getty Images; 2, Nattika/Shutterstock; 3, syolacan/Getty Images; 4, Jesse Estes/Getty Images; 5, Sombat Muycheen/Shutterstock; 6, Andrej Safaric/Shutterstock; 7, Fiesta Photography/Shutterstock; 8, Colin Anderson/Getty Images; 9, Lora Liu/Shutterstock; 10, Julia Davila-Lampe/Getty Images; 11, Ondrej Prosicky/Shutterstock; 12, va103/Getty Images; 13, Ondrej Prosicky/Shutterstock; 14, Boris Stroujko/Shutterstock; 15, Matt Propert; 16, Xiangfeng Xu/EyeEm/Getty Images; 17, studio on line/Shutterstock; 18, Denis Belitsky/Shutterstock; 19, Studio 37/Shutterstock; 20, Minerva Studio/Getty Images; 21, drpnncpptak/Shutterstock; 22, Neale Cousland/Shutterstock; 23, Alan Dyer/Stocktrek Images/Getty Images; 24, Sara Winter/Shutterstock; 25, bluesky85/Getty Images; 26, Sharon Cobo/Shutterstock; 27, Olivia Bell Photography/Getty Images; 28, Susannah Photography/Getty Images; 29, Clement Kiragu/Shutterstock; 30, Waddell Images/Shutterstock.

October

Opener, crossbrain66/Getty Images; 1, kuvona/Shutterstock; 2, Dimitrios Tilis/Getty Images; 3, Stacey Newman/Getty Images; 4, Tomas Sereda/Getty Images; 5, Paul_K/Shutterstock; 6, Serge Skiba/Shutterstock; 7, Kevin van der Leek Photography/Getty Images; 8, RRuntsch/Shutterstock; 9, corgarashu/Shutterstock; 10, kertlis/Getty Images; 11, Niki van Velden/Getty Images; 12, Ales Krivec/Shutterstock; 13, Baitong/Shutterstock; 14, Quinn Miller-Bedell/National Geographic Your Shot; 15, Michael Nichols/National Geographic Creative; 16, Melory/Shutterstock; 17, A. Basler/Shutterstock; 18, Luxx Images/Getty Images; 19, Kochergin/Getty Images; 20, Sandra Caldwell/Shutterstock; 21, Matt Propert; 22, jahmaica/Getty Images; 23, Matt Propert; 24, Ondrej Prosicky/Shutterstock; 25, Javier Brosch/Shutterstock; 26, Family Business/Shutterstock; 27, Anettphoto/Shutterstock; 28, Andrew Mayovskyy/Shutterstock; 29, nito/Shutterstock; 30, Matt Propert; 31, Matt Propert.

November

Opener, Naphat Photography/Getty Images; 1, freya-photographer/Shutterstock; 2, Michael Nichols/National Geographic Creative; 3, Welcome to MichaelAnthonyImages at Getty Images; 4, Carole Gomez/Getty Images; 5, borchee/Getty Images; 6, MirageC/Getty Images; 7, vichie81/Shutterstock; 8, qingqing/Shutterstock; 9, Julia Smith/Getty Images; 10, Eric Isselee/Shutterstock; 11, Andrew Mayovskyy/Shutterstock; 12, Andrew Mayovskyy/Shutterstock; 13, Martin Ruegner/Getty Images; 14, sbaines/Getty Images; 15, stockstudioX/Getty Images; 16, twomeows/Getty Images; 17, Africa Studio/Shutterstock; 18, mama_mia/Shutterstock; 19, irin-k/Shutterstock; 20, Lifebrary/Shutterstock; 21, David Alan Harvey/National Geographic Creative; 22, FEBRUARY/Getty Images; 23, Colin Varndell/Nature Picture Library/Getty Images; 24, Mikadun/Shutterstock; 25, Kan Khampanya/Shutterstock; 26, Matt Propert; 27, My Good Images/Shutterstock; 28, Todd Klassy/Shutterstock; 29, Sam Abell/National Geographic Creative; 30, Creaturart Images/Shutterstock.

December

Opener, borchee/Getty Images; 1, nevereverro/Getty Images; 2, John Glade/Shutterstock; 3, Maxim Khytra/Shutterstock; 4, Songsak P/Shutterstock; 5, Sylvie Corriveau/Shutterstock; 6, JFunk/Shutterstock; 7, Anna-Mari West/Shutterstock; 8, kiboka/Shutterstock; 9, David Clapp/Getty Images; 10, George F. Mobley/National Geographic Creative; 11, Creative Travel Projects/Shutterstock; 12, Sergei Borisevich/Shutterstock; 13, Per Breiehagen/Getty Images; 14, I wave/Shutterstock; 15, tomertu/Shutterstock; 16, Alexandra King/Shutterstock; 17, Creative Travel Projects/Shutterstock; 18, Vilor/Shutterstock; 19, jakkapan/Shutterstock; 20, Viktar Dzerkach/Shutterstock; 21, Vlad Ozerov/Shutterstock; 22, wingmar/Getty Images; 23, rdonar/Shutterstock; 24, Alexandr Iurochkin/Shutterstock; 25, Anna Pustynnikova/Shutterstock; 26, Michael Thaler/Shutterstock; 27, borchee/Getty Images; 28, Joyce Marrero/Shutterstock; 29, Leonid Ikan/Shutterstock; 30, Nature Photography/Shutterstock; 31, [Genesis]—Korawee Ratchapakdee/Getty Images.

Credits, Jesse Estes/Getty Images.

ACKNOWLEDGMENTS

Daily Kindness would not have been possible without the hard work of the wonderful National Geographic team: senior editor Hilary Black, project editors Allyson Dickman and Anne Smyth, researchers Lindsay Anderson and Kris Heitkamp, designer Katie Olsen, assistant designer Callie Bonaccorsy, design production coordinator Nicole Miller, photo editor Uliana Bazar, production editor Judith Klein, and countless others who gave their time and talent to this book.

READ.
BREATHE.
FEEL.

Experience all of life's pleasures with daily doses of inspiration and mindfulness. In these beautiful books, stunning photographs are paired with meaningful reflections that will uplift and nurture you every day of the year.

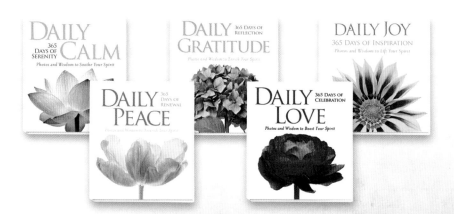

DAILY CALM
365 DAYS OF SERENITY
Photos and Wisdom to Soothe Your Spirit

DAILY GRATITUDE
365 DAYS OF REFLECTION
Photos and Wisdom to Enrich Your Spirit

DAILY JOY
365 DAYS OF INSPIRATION
Photos and Wisdom to Lift Your Spirit

DAILY PEACE
365 DAYS OF RENEWAL
Photos and Wisdom to Awaken Your Spirit

DAILY LOVE
365 DAYS OF CELEBRATION
Photos and Wisdom to Boost Your Spirit